Other Books by George Kalamaras

POETRY

That Moment of Wept (2018)

The Hermit's Way of Being Human (2015)

The Mining Camps of the Mouth (2012)

Kingdom of Throat-Stuck Luck (2011)

Symposium on the Body's Left Side (2011)

Your Own Ox-Head Mask as Proof (2010)

The Recumbent Galaxy (2010)
(with Alvaro Cardona-Hine)

Something Beautiful Is Always Wearing the Trees (2009)
(with paintings by Alvaro Cardona-Hine)

The Scathering Sound (2009)

Gold Carp Jack Fruit Mirrors (2008)

Even the Java Sparrows Call Your Hair (2004)

Borders My Bent Toward (2003)

The Theory and Function of Mangoes (2000)

Beneath the Breath (1988)

Heart Without End (1986)

CRITICISM

Reclaiming the Tacit Dimension: Symbolic Form in the Rhetoric of Silence (1994)

LUMINOUS IN THE OWL'S RIB

GEORGE KALAMARAS

2019

DOS MADRES PRESS, INC.
P.O. Box 294, Loveland, Ohio 45140
www.dosmadres.com   editor@dosmadres.com

Dos Madres is dedicated to the belief that the small press is essential to the vitality of contemporary literature as a carrier of the new voice, as well as the older, sometimes forgotten voices of the past. And in an ever more virtual world, to the creation of fine books pleasing to the eye and hand.

Dos Madres is named in honor of Vera Murphy and Libbie Hughes, the "Dos Madres" whose contributions have made this press possible.

Dos Madres Press, Inc. is an Ohio Not For Profit Corporation and a 501 (c) (3) qualified public charity. Contributions are tax deductible.

Executive Editor: Robert J. Murphy

Book Design: Elizabeth H. Murphy
www.illusionstudios.net

Author photo: Jim Whitcraft

Cover image: Wood engraving on off-white wove paper by William Blake, "Blasted Tree and Flattened Crops," from *The Pastorals of Virgil*, 1821, William McCallin McKee Memorial Endowment (The Art Institute of Chicago)

Typeset in Adobe Garamond Pro & Cochin
ISBN 978-1-948017-61-9
Library of Congress Control Number: 2019947316

First Edition
Copyright 2019 George Kalamaras

All rights reserved. No part of this book may be reproduced or transmitted in any form or by any means graphic, electronic or mechanical, including photo-copying, recording, taping or by any information storage or retrieval system, without the permission in writing from the publisher.

Published by Dos Madres Press, Inc.

ACKNOWLEDGMENTS

I want to thank the editors of the following in which nearly all of these poems, or their previous versions, first appeared:

Abiko Quarterly (Japan): "Worms" (winner of the *Abiko Quarterly* International Poetry Prize)
American Letters & Commentary: "The Little Tear Gland That Says Tic Tac"
Barnstorm: "The Trouble with Being Human"
Blue Mesa Review: "Track of the World, the Cup Holds No Crow"
Boulevard: "A History of Green"
Calibanonline: "Night Dreamer" and "Everybody Digs Bill Evans"
Dispatches from the Poetry Wars: "The Sound Behind Water," "The Book of Dandelions," "A History," "You Slice Away All That Is Not Vowel," "After Ray Gonzalez and I Read Our Poetry, Our Friend Bill Tremblay Complements Our Reading," and "It's Gone"
Down to the Dark River: Poems about the Mississippi River (Louisiana Literature Press): "Please, Rain-in-My-Throat"
The Drunken Boat: "And Finally, the Brides of Lust" (as part of an online chapbook, *The Transformation of Salt*)
ELF: Eclectic Literary Forum: "Entering the Corridors of Breath"
Gargoyle: "Tonight at the Five Spot" (print issue), "Fernando Pessoa Might Call My Body True" (print issue), and "Buhaina" (audio CD issue)
Hotel Amerika: "Wes Montgomery's Autopsy," "The Pharmaceutical Chemist to Whom Sailors Came to Get Their Shiners Leeched," and "Map Points"

Hopewell Review: Indiana's Best Writers: "Woman Handing Man an Envelope, Chinese Servant with Moth Wings, Standing on a Floor of Water"
I Just Wanna Testify: Poems About Detroit Music (Michigan State University Press): "Every Note You Play Is a Blue Note"
The Little Magazine: "Evening Raga"
Malpaís Review: "Had I Had a Daughter Named Delia" and "The Translation of Gratitude"
The Main Street Rag: "Bangkok Fan (from a Brother Monk)"
Maize: "Smaller Than What"
Map Points: "Dreaming Oneself Dead"
Midwest Quarterly: "The Bell Tree"
Origin: "What Love?" and "Lee Morgan: The Sidewinder"
Pemmican: "Elegy for McGrath"
Pomegranate Seeds: An Anthology of Greek-American Poetry (Somerset Hall Press): "On the Death of Miltos Sahtouris"
River Styx: "Hiroshima as Inscribed in the Book of Questions"
Sentence: A Journal of Prose Poetics: "Francis Ponge Is on Fire"
Shade: "Luminous in the Owl's Rib"
Shaking Like a Mountain: "Tina Brooks, Live at Smalls Paradise, April 1958"
Solo Café: "Frumkin Seeds"
Taos Journal of Poetry & Art: "Wake This Red. Drink the Reach of Grief"
Ur-Vox: "Mingus Mingus Mingus"
Yen Agat (Thailand): "House and Universe"

Gratitude to Rabbit Light Videos and filmmaker Joshua Marie Wilkerson for producing the short film (with my reading of the poem), "The Voice of George Kalamaras"

I also wish to thank the following for reprinting some of the preceding poems in their pages:

And Know This Place: Poetry of Indiana (Indiana Historical Society): "A History of Green"
AnthologY: Visiting Authors, 2006 (The Writer's Voice of the YMCA of Greater Syracuse): "A History of Green" and "The Bell Tree"
The Best American Poetry 2009 (Scribner): "Francis Ponge Is on Fire"
The Bitter Oleander: "Worms" (first North American reprint)
The Chicago Blues Guide: "Entering the Corridors of Breath"
"Eating the Pure Light": Homage to Thomas McGrath (The Backwaters Press): "Elegy for McGrath"
Indiana Humanities Council Website: "A History of Green"
Kiss the Sky: Fiction and Poetry Starring Jimi Hendrix (Paycock Press): "Entering the Corridors of Breath"
New Voices: Poetry and Fiction from Colorado State University (The Center for Literary Publishing, Colorado State University): "Evening Raga"
No More Corn: Indiana's Laureate on Hoosier Poets (website of former poet laureate, Karen Kovacik): "A History of Green"

Grateful acknowledgment, as well, to Longhouse Publishers for printing a limited edition poetry pamphlet, *Mingus Mingus Mingus*, in which the following appeared for the first time: "For Max Roach" and "Blue Bossa," and in which the following were reprinted: "What Love?" "Buhaina," "Lee Morgan: The Sidewinder," and "Mingus Mingus Mingus"

Gratitude to Tilton House Press (Denver, Colorado) for printing the chapbook *Beneath the Breath*, in which "Entering the Corridors of Breath" appeared.

I want to thank my wife, Mary Ann Cain, for her unending inspiration and support, as we share our lives, work, and love. I'm also immensely grateful to John Bradley for his thoughtful and generous commentary on my poems, none of which would be the same without all we share. Huge thanks, as well, goes to Eric Baus, Joseph Gastiger, Ray Gonzalez, Patrick Lawler, Jennifer Militello, Paul B. Roth, and Lawrence R. Smith. No acknowledgment would be complete, however, without honoring the life and teachings of Paramahansa Yogananda. I am remarkably rich with influences and friends.

TABLE OF CONTENTS

A DAUGHTER NAMED DELIA

Had I Had a Daughter Named Delia — 1

FIERCE AND FULL OF MENDING

The Sound Behind Water — 5
A History of Green — 6
The Bell Tree — 8
For Max Roach — 9
Tonight at the Five Spot — 11
Please, Rain-in-My-Throat — 13
Bangkok Fan (from a Brother Monk) — 15
The Trouble with Being Human — 17
Woman Handing Man an Envelope, Chinese Servant
    with Moth Wings, Standing on a Floor of Water — 19

FOR THE NOT-YET DEAD

Hiroshima as Inscribed in the Book of Questions — 25
Track of the World, the Cup Holds No Crow — 29
The Little Tear Gland That Says Tic Tac — 30
Wes Montgomery's Autopsy — 32
What Love? — 35
Dreaming Oneself Dead — 38
On the Death of Miltos Sahtouris — 40
Francis Ponge Is on Fire — 43
Fernando Pessoa Might Call My Body True — 44

CHROMIUM BONES AND IMPERFECT PRECISION

Every Note You Play Is a Blue Note — 49
Tina Brooks, Live at Smalls Paradise, April 1958 — 52
Buhaina — 55
The Book of Dandelions — 57
Elegy for McGrath — 60
Frumkin Seeds — 62
The Pharmaceutical Chemist to Whom Sailors
    Came to Get Their Shiners Leeched — 65
And Finally, the Brides of Lust — 67
Worms — 69

LOST IN THE ANIMAL

Luminous in the Owl's Rib — 75
Map Points — 76
Blue Bossa — 77
Lee Morgan: The Sidewinder — 78
A History — 80
You Slice Away All That Is Not Vowel — 83
After Ray Gonzalez and I Read Our Poetry, Our Friend
    Bill Tremblay Complements Our Reading — 84
The Urologist's Daughter — 86
The Voice of George Kalamaras — 88

WE, AMONG THE LIVING

Wake This Red. Drink the Reach of Grief — 93
Night Dreamer — 96
Everybody Digs Bill Evans — 98
Mingus Mingus Mingus — 100
It's Gone — 102
Smaller Than What — 104
House and Universe — 105
Entering the Corridors of Breath — 106
Evening Raga — 109

HOW NOW THE SCAR

The Translation of Gratitude — 113

Notes — 117
About the Author — 121

for Mary Ann and Bootsie

*and in memory of my mother,
Georgina H. Allen—the first one
to give me music*

"Love and hunger—that is my whole story."

—Thomas McGrath

A Daughter Named Delia

Had I Had a Daughter Named Delia

Had I had a daughter I would have named her *Delia*.
Nobody names their sons *George* anymore.

The name *Delia* contains the sway of a dark fluid flower.
Nobody names their daughters *Delia* anymore.

Had I a fish, I would have called it *belovèd whopping cough to which I am inscribed*.
Nobody calls their coughs tenderly anymore.

Had I loved a fig, I would have called it *certain lovely fig in the now of my mouth*.
No one describes the mouthed-now of *lovely* anymore.

Had Delia and I been father and daughter, I would have held her fever, clutched her daily dissolve, taught her the invisible, all the ways of softness I know, even how to release that certain vulnerable hunch she'd no doubt inherit from my own childhood strain.
No one teaches touch anymore, a way to kiss the inside bleeding of a star, anymore.

Had Delia asked me, *Dad, I don't understand boys. I am unsure of my sway, the mood of my moon—how can I rejoice?* I would have named her *normal*.
No one is named *normal* anymore.

Had I had a daughter named *Delia*, I would have loved

her *just* for being my daughter, asked her to name *her* daughter Delia too.

At least not when you're sixty-three and male and childless and male, nobody names their daughter's daughter anymore.

Fierce and Full of Mending

The Sound Behind Water

People are always asking, *Which house is this?*
They open a door, and my chest sprouts sparrows
They close a window as an avocado dirts to seed
They look for the outline of a tree in fog
It is barely there, behind their water
Beneath the sky
Inside the grass
Is a shape that moves like an eel
In the marsh of your eyes
I see myself struggling for sound
Like a hermit who, even after years of silence,
Can't forget his own name
We are struck to the earth like a bar of scented soap
An egret who has grown an extra leg
I move hesitantly, feeling a larger portion of the world
Weighing less than a ballroom without snow
I float further into myself
Like a clock narrowing as it leaves midnight
Like a thin rug that has taken many years to weave

A History of Green

Green is for growth, fatigue, Fort Wayne, Indiana,
spring. The burgundy of a smoke tree
slosh against horse chestnut and oak.
The centipede's blood, *that* green, incursion of lust.
The dark Aegean loneliness of Nikos Gatsos
green. Cricket scratch tugging anemic green
before the rain-stoked sky. Spark-stacked might,
the lightning green of an unbloomed lilac bush.
Light*en*ing green of haloes of violet
at first bloom of the infant's crown at birth.
Banaras green of sunset oxcarts, that lull
in a monk's left foot mesmerizing Ganges River green.
The paleness of curds cut by lemon juice
from goat or water-buffalo milk. The sudden gash
of aged cheese, of sun-bit trees, of the hosta back home
bowing darkened with cloud-crowded May.
The Stilton green of dead English smells.
Colonized fruit stalls in Jammu
and Rangoon. Mung bean, yarrow green, bulrush
and reed. The scent of her clarinet
breast through bamboo. The momentary green
of all the water in the world
and how everyone is everybody else
in a freshly shaved underarm
as she reaches for a dish or cup.
The Saturn turn of complete nothingness,
and your tongue stands scars
where might a star. Green of the circus tent
telling the juggler *yes* or *no* or *maybe one day
so*. Not just three or four pears in the air

green. Not the torn planet of sliced avocado
seed green. Nor Nikos or, even, Gatsos green.
But Lorca green. Trench-lip green. Willow smoke
of motorcycle skid, husky green Granada.
The momentary Gobi retracted green
of every desert in the whirl. Even the year
1936 backhoed below sumac
shade of 1963 Indiana green, of all things
in reverse. The way Franco green
throws away the key, retreats
to repeat itself in black,
in blue. Green wanting green
wanting green (yes, Miguel Hernández green)
to fall its onion tentacle shade-shift
self all the way through the earth
as an echo of ferns reaching further
into the glandular girth
of fetterless starlight. Fade back,
that is, to a great pulsing
galactic placental green, before love
or color, touch or color, tongue or
color. A great ghost-got green
far away from dark sound light
sound tuberculous seed, from *this* and *that*,
yes and *no*, from, even,
maybe one day so.

The Bell Tree

She holds a celadon bowl and he
a hole in his shirt cuff. Or is it
his shoulder? Sitting, so similar to standing
or, in the lap, folding hands in fragrance
after a fight. The single dark elm
with its glowing bark. A lantern
swinging like underwater speech. What is slow
is slower than the color green repairing
itself below November fields. Than a hair-
line crack in a bowl, fierce
and full of mending. Stars drain
their slivery deaths in the spark
of bells. It is Sunday
and the need for church. Or it is
Saturday, the tendency for touch or tongue.
Stitch or web of dewy moonlight in the hole
toward the shoulder or, in that openness
that spans the rim of a bowl
left out to inherit rain, certain
fragments of color. Or it is Tuesday
and the desire for soup, anything remotely moist
from the various openings
of the body, so often clothed.
Whose mouth is whose when they speak,
when they kiss? When one nose nudges
the urge of another? As if trying to reach
through the rough bark, toughing it out
in themselves in tongues too dark
and distant, in curves of loss
and more loss. Planing the rough edges
of starlight. Clanging the bells.

For Max Roach

Sky-tilt as if the world girthed seed.
Circumference of sound retracting to its center.
Minefield of autonomy elegantly placed.
Spaces between notes having a hand in your sad.

All this, spoken of, fought, brought to bounce
fire between beats. Roach man, you crawled light
through us. Whether with Clifford, George Morrow,
or even your self clear as husk,

you musked us into the pounding of our own
strain. An African hedgehog circumambulates
the feces of flamingos? A lift of color,
like a slowly ripped curtain, graces

the lake with depths of chloritic pink?
Gorillas, when autopsied, reveal a zebra
heart, confirm that the color of love
from which we've revolved is neither black nor white?

Love, you told us, *is a many splendored thing*
somehow splintering off with the back beat
you've become. They say one day only sharks
and roaches will inhabit the earth. That we grow

into our names. That if you're named *George*,
for instance, you'll feel and act like a king. Roach, man,
you're more than a scuttling of timpani
when the light goes out. More than the seeking

of woodwork when it snaps back on,
guiding you into your next life. I don't
feel like a king—and maybe neither did
Morrow—that is, until I hear your smooth groove

me back before speech to the drumbeat
of word girthing word, attempting to color-birth
sound out of the roundness of now. Two sticks
in your hand, Max. Fire our speech-smog with song.

Tonight at the Five Spot

So I'm listening to Kenny Burrell
and Art Blakey tonight from the Five Spot.
The opening cut, Dizzy's "Birk's Works."
And I'm hearing the other music
in the background—applause after each
solo, clink of glass, the tabletop
tones tapped out by a stranger's grooving
hand. Bobby Timmons lays the keys, tells me
piano notes are possum tracks back to late August
nights, 1959. Whose birthday
was on the twenty-fifth? And did she feel young
again when Blakey stroked the skins, safely
tucked in the marsupial pouch of night?
Now the treatment of a dump truck pours sand
back through the spiderwebbed throat of a guy
at the bar, hunched from the load work left
dented into him, too soon to go home.
What was missing in his life, sucked upon
in scotch on the rocks sipped slow between tracks?
Kenny must already be missing
Sonny Clark, though he wouldn't overdose
for another three years. He could read future
sorrow each time he bent back a chord,
as if a tarot of notes charged toll,
the strings of his guitar like the digits
on a mortician's hand counting out
all the Lee-Morgan dead—those hard-bit dudes
who tried to kick the Horse but got kicked
in the head instead, crueling their duel
with youth. All possible dead air this night

are lungfish wallowing in the mud
in Tina Brooks's sax. Five-fingered count
says he'll only record two years more.
Says the Five Spot is a Lincoln palmed
from a friend but also the waiting dead
already there in the background awe
of the crowd's applause. How many patrons,
even, are still alive? Did they dodge disease?
Were they given the death of a cat?
Did they return to this joint night after night
to hear their lives slip past? This five-piece band
reaches beyond the grasp of death's hand, saying,
*Spot me five. Let me buy a nickel bag,
my brother. I got the itch, and there ain't
no Junk. Let me calm myself, buy some time
with five tokes through the five steady steeples
of the hand.* What is the sound of one man
dying? What are the tones, the minor notes,
dizzying me tonight, from a café
fifty-five years late? How can this music
keep slipping me some skin from the hard life
of these sorrowful men surrounded by fives
at the Five Spot, on the twenty-fifth
day of August, in 1959—
not in New York but Indiana this time,
Fort Wayne, in the almost-light of five a.m.?

Please, Rain-in-My-Throat

Bad Axe River. Kaskaskia. The Ohio, which connects to
Indiana's Wabash. For 411 miles the Wabash tumbles
undammed, like 400 or more names for the wandering tribes
of Ishmael, slipped from leaves of sassafras and willow.

That dream where marsupials from New Guinea populate
the Mississippi River Valley. Upper Basin, Lower Basin. And
possums, the only marsupial in the Western hemisphere, eat
insects from timber-fall rotting along the Mississippi. Eat insects
that somehow thrive all the way from Borneo and Tasmania.

The French and Indian War was really about control of
Pennsylvania. Which was about control of the Ohio Valley.
Which was about control of each insect bite on the arms of
fur traders along the sinkholes and drift of the Mississippi.

If I dreamed beaver pelt and sash, would you say names of
the Mississippi hidden in the soft under-throat of hound
dogs that tree game in the lantern-lit woods sloping toward
the cricket-thick night?

Maquoketa River. Marys River. Menomenee. Three names for three or more ways of mouth oaring into the pores of the doe-eyed Mississippi.

So you died. So I felt like dying. So on that day blue jays became robins. Robins became ring-necked pheasants. Pheasants, hawks. Hawks, a tiny pine mouse shivering in a hollow tree stump along the Wabash. The Kankakee. Among Hay Creek and the Galena River in Illinois. Blackhawk track. Moccasin blood along footpaths of the Mississippi.

There is always a war of words inside the mouth when it tries to say simple things like *river* or *drain-into-my-heart*. How to keep one river separate from another? How to keep life from depth? Word from blur? Better to speak it slantwise as rain in the throat. Better to bury it, with the possum-pup dead, with the heart and viscera of a white-tailed deer, at the foot of a shagbark hickory in a ritual of *Please, Rain-in-My-Throat.*

If I named you, I could call you only *death*. If I killed my naming of you. If I killed it and quivered and quick. I could claim you were a river. Many rivers. The rumbling of water over rock. Of rock over silt. Of silt sanding the fossilized plants of Indiana somehow buried among the split and drift, the moist and mud. The age and ache of the Mississippi.

Bangkok Fan (from a Brother Monk)

for Thomas Merton

At that time, he wrote movingly of loss.
Electricity had come to our hermitage.
He had slept soundly before it came,
the photons in his body completely
aligned. Now, he had told us,
it felt good to go a few days
without speaking a word. Despite his relief,
cabbage leaves from the monastery
soup still haunted him, even in radio
sleep he remembered from childhood.
It was unlike a dream, more like loving
the smell of tea while sitting on the rectory sofa.
Perhaps I was right. Perhaps my meditations
had, from afar, stirred his sooty sleep.
There had been a candle, a large black boot,
a sudden twist of wind. Wet autumn leaves
dampened their hands across his view. He had gone
East in 1968, studied Theravada Buddhism
in Wat Bovoranives before moving onto
Calcutta. Yes, the Bangkok fan was still
in his future, five and a half months
ahead, like a mass of breeding breaths turning
its twisted tail in self-made wind. *What is
important*, Merton had told us, *is not liberation
from the body but liberation
from the mind. We are not entangled
in our own body but entangled
in our own mind.* We heard him talk once in Calcutta
on the monk as a "marginal" person. We returned

to Bangkok with him, heard him lecture lovingly
that morning on "Marxism and Monastic
Perspectives." Yes, we had lunch afterwards,
and when he retired to his room
for a shower and nap, we heard a pop,
then a shout, then the radio-slurp
of December 10 grogging our veins
toward almost-complete sleep. At the end
of the meridian, one of our brother monks
who found his body on the floor received a shock
himself when removing the still-turning fan
from Merton's naked, freshly washed chest
but was probably saved, we later learned, by wearing shoes.

The Trouble with Being Human

It seemed secure as a proper-fitting shoe.
Then the cabbage soup got cold.

We leaned into our autumn evening
and disturbed the owl, somehow there
in the kitchen, perfectly content
by the pot. Mostly, though,
our breath was gypsy.

We touched a pair of candles.
Great wagons with torches came
toward us. The smell of Transylvanian pine
resin and flame. Long shadows
larger and smaller than a bark canoe
that swept past, containing our secret.

What grain of love grew in the unkind word?
In the public coat and collar-turning
against the mold that collected just as anemic
green in other people's plates?
What was in the bone of the hand that made it
reach toward another, shake vigorously
upon meeting some stranger? The rivers in the palm
were no help. Once, mine even read
Trouble ahead at the same time as
You are a perfect soul.

What restrained the breath,
made it lift and fall
even in our sleep, as if some star-filled

indigo ocean struggled against our will to flood
the prairie with the piracy of our dream?

The soup contained tomato and leeks
and, of course, requisite slabs
of cabbage. It recalled deep forest,
Hungarian ponies, and dark rye,
tasted vaguely of pine cone
and the resinous sadness
of the poems of Lucian Blaga.

We listened to the dwindling dancing fire
snap of Saturday evening
radio talk, clung like salve
to the list of jazz lions
after each cut.

We fed the owl tiny roasted seeds
that seemed to come from *us*.
Asked its forgiveness
for what, as human, we had done
just to stay alive.
For what hurt lay ahead
that we might, unknowingly, one day do.

Woman Handing Man an Envelope, Chinese Servant with Moth Wings, Standing on a Floor of Water

based on a collage by Max Ernst

At 5:05 he leaves the bank where he works, walks
into the parlor three and a half blocks from where

the train dropped him. She hands him the envelope,
breaking the seal. A cone of light opens

on the wall. Words pour out into *left* and *right*,
yes and *no*. Something in the room is shifting.

Still, he stands erect in his dark brown suit.
Something in his servant's sash reminds him

of a June night, even on the eleventh moon
of the eleventh harp, a vague stirring

of moths in his silk. Was it a garter snake
he saw in the hedgerow outside the bank? Her blue bodice

and secret slip? A touch of yellow tanager?
Some vague green star? She cannot be said

even in the telling of it. He once drew
with an orange crayon a mare

with fierce fetlock and mane. Drew,
years later, his wife's skirts above her

waist, heard moths struggle in the candle
of her eye, saw lightning, that is, in the shape

of startled rope. Two tongues entwined in June.
It's easy for him, even as they stand on a parlor floor

that's dissolving now like the names they once had
for one another, names like *hope* and *touch* and

Emma-who-will-one-day-grow-up-to-play-the-piano,
a living room of melting ice. And how her song presses

on him with tufts of feathers
from an owl's chest. A mannequin,

in a storefront, in sequined stockings and heels—
a watery word—hands him an envelope

with official seal. And he bows, deeply, like any man
who owes a swan. A tiger prowls

through his night sweats, through the smoky sleep
of a Chinese servant who, downstairs in secret,

puffs perfect smoke rings through him, and a starfish comes
to his chest. And the brown of his mother's eyes

enters the sound of his groin. A music lesson
never learned. Tea without orange flower

water. Wallpaper in the attitude of the roses
of the dead. She stands each day in the parlor

at precisely 5:13, hands him an envelope
that is always empty, that always contains a lock

of young hair. A floor that turns
to water whenever she is near.

For the
Not-Yet
Dead

Hiroshima as Inscribed
in the Book of Questions

How could it have happened like that,
in our own ears
among the vowel
and split
of isotropic drift?

How could it have happened
in the Midwest
among crickets and dusk
and moist teenage tongues urging
the right kind of rubbing
to ignite rows of moonlight in the corn?

How could we ever return
to North
and West
and South,
to the calm of Chesterfields
in our lungs, without first feeling
the sudden vapor of ants
blurring the air
in our tubes?

We could travel a thousand molecules
of the holy Ganges
inside the spine
and barely lift that lightning

dawn from the coiled mouth
of the serpent.

We could go east in our own pants
and never feel full again
where we want to hold it the most.

We could twirl our skirts and pumps
around gypsy fire
and forever fear
our heat.

On that bright summer day,
it is written,
Harry S. Truman slung
his head in his hands, ashamed
of Mr. and Mrs. Gray, of Baby Gray,
and Baby Gray's secret dawn decoder
ring, and that friendly panting collie.

On that bald-bright day,
it is written,
Benito Mussolini
rose at dawn
from his gallows-stiffened body,
gathered his disciples
about him, and—kissing
Mary Magdalene on the lips—ascended
to his Father, weeping
for that lost thread

of his own left sock
left behind in the hamper.

On that starry-bright day,
it is written,
Vincent Van Gogh repeatedly refused
the advances of trash collectors
to return his lettuce-leaf
ear. Couldn't hear the flash
of zebra fish going sunflower-
orange, a moment, before
touching the extremities of ash.
Couldn't paint, that is, their skeletal
sound. *It is finished*, they hummed
into the deaf August dissolve,
and then pumping their gills, sighed,
but where's the vinegar?

*How could it have ever happened
like that? All I really wanted
was a thirteenth disciple*, Benito wept,
*a little summer home
on the coast of Sicily, some bread
and wine, a good long
woman, and a faithful left sock.*

How could it have happened?
Harry thought. *In August, like that,
with the Grays taking snapshots
at Yosemite, and my wife*

*in gaucho pants
beneath cherry blossoms
in rain.*

How could it happen? Vincent kept repeating,
rummaging, on hands and knees,
through the dump outside of town.
*All I wanted was to hear
something sunflower-gold.
All I ever wanted was love.*

Track of the World, the Cup Holds No Crow

The wind moves the way a boy drinks green tea.
All at once crows emerge from the gardener's belly.
The man (*what* man?) arrives on the train (*which* train?)
and begins to place wood shavings from his newspaper
into the bottom of the cup. Dandelions blossom
in the yard, in the field, among the gardener
and the crow. All the bellies (*what* bellies?)
of the world (*which* vowel?) begin to calm soybean
vibrations of the thorax acting like a crow
searching its wing for air. Searching the train
(*what* train?) for news (*which* food?), the man (*what* calm?)
drinks a cup of dandelion (tea?). All at once
a boy emerges from his belly, in the train, in the field,
among the tracks and snow (*what* snow?). It's cold,
and wind flowers down flakes of burnt white skin.
All the crows (*what* train?) of the belly (*which* shavings?)
ease up through the thorax like the slip of a tempered
voice. The bottom of the cup. Dandelions. Crow shout.
Search the cup for a tea leaf, souchong, and news
of the porcelain grip, the laying by aching men
(*which* thorax?) of the track.

The Little Tear Gland That Says Tic Tac
based on a painting by Max Ernst

The Chinese emperor has black tea in his eyes.
More Lapsong Souchong? his servant asks.

The little tear gland that says tic tac
says *tic tac. Oh*, says the servant.

You want a lemon wedge too! Outside
courtyard gates, the blue wheel of a tractor

is loose in the sky, becoming the boomerang
wind around which a willow forms. The imperial

falconer strokes the throat of his tercel,
instructing it on the virtues of earth.

The palace horticulturist scrapes telium
into a porcelain cup, sips bits of rust

and black tea, contemplates in the courtyard
the vulva of a sow. *To cry for once*

just to cry, just to feel the lips of a kiss
cut glass chrysanthemums into your cheek,

just to feel gravel rakes of a Zen garden
scratch a smooth rooster strut

out of your tear ducts! He wonders
if a person's blood after tea has the bend

of hydrangeas, the texture of rust. *Yes,*
gestures the emperor to his servant with a lift

of his left wrist. The gold bell of his sleeve
summons the court when he removes an eyelash

with the heron-beak nail of his right index finger.
The little tear gland that says tic tac says *tic tac.*

Wes Montgomery's Autopsy

So we introduced Epsom salts into the lower calf.
So we excised the initials from his gold
money clip, implanting them in his chest.
So we tested the weight of his heart
with spitting contests until we reached the far wall.
So we confused his name, *Wes*, with the great
outdoors. Began planning trips *Out Wes*,
ventured to the video store and requested
Wes Side Story and *How the Wes Was Won*.
So we realized his guitar made him
not just a Hoosier from Indianapolis
but a gunslinger not unlike Eustace,
that fast-smoking ukulele kid.
And so we peeled back the left eyelid
which revealed a guitar pick the color of euxenite.
And when we let his blood into the cup
the janitor swore he could see starlings
evacuate each of our right ears.

                                    How many smokes
later did we decide to collect his cells
and place them on a slide? How many smokes
a day had he consumed, and how did they
relate to the freckled pigmentation
near his face? In Ethiopia,
pond scum is viewed as a delicacy
with which to gravy cooked grain? In Mozambique,
the color green is said to bless the frogs
with strange unripened fruit spots
on the pelican part of their necks?

And so we interspersed ourselves, spittle
drop by spittle drop, into his lowest bowel.
And so we exercised our tongues in his
left ear. And so we claimed his body
as our own, the cattle drive West from Indy
as our dark embrace of the Lewis and Clark view.
And so all this we thought we dreamed, manifestly,
though we had been awake a long time,
at least since the first hurt, since being human,
since the childhood scoldings had unavoidably closed our mouths.

Gunslinger slinging his smokin' six-string tired town
to tired town—live at the Tsubo in Berkeley,
sets at Stillwater, Red Lodge, and San Antone,
some smoky dive in Dodge or Abilene.
We found the pineal gland and drank deeply
thereof. In opening what he'd kept closed,
we caught our breath
again and again. In our esophageal haze,
we inherited fragments of his memory still fidgeting carp
snap from his brain. After each gig—
we could see through half-lit amber,
twitching still from nerve pools
in his wrist—he'd lie
on his bed, delicately smoke, pull
back his shirts to reveal dead birds,
his eye, for an instant, fluttering
heavenward. Through the body
of the dead, we could drink, *see*,
hold those private images from his hotel smoke.
He'd remember his axe, it seemed,

in the corner in a case singing
like a holster's leather-snap crack. Callous-growth
still creased from pressing the strings.
And smoke—gun smoke resin on his hand—
from buckshotting in some bar
the sidewinder glance of his fans?
His finger still stinging from our need.

What Love?

for Eric Dolphy

I said I wouldn't bleed, promised my insides
each sunset to the blood orange at the sink,

my all-that-is-in-me to the bowl of pears.
But Antibes, over and again,

and your bass clarinet on all thirteen
minutes thirty-four seconds of "What Love?"

Your just-about-to-die breath holding up
not only Curson's trumpet and Booker on tenor

but the sad weight of Mingus at fifty-six. Dolphy,
what gives, brother, in the final reflex of your eye?

Is it true that when Mingus died in Cuernavaca, fifty-six
whales beached themselves that day on the Mexican coast?

That when *you* passed, no one was there to see
sparrows spill out, lovingly, from the ossicles

of your ear? Mantra *diksha* is always given
in the right as one way to hold the self's dissolve.

As a means of hobbling the young
camels of Rajasthan? Of oiling

tree branches in Sri Lanka bending over
the supposed graves of Cain and Abel?

I said I, told myself, even begged
the color orange, promising the pears

the moist that might gentle my bite. But it's hard,
Dolph—this stutter-dove 'bout as thrust

as the stomach of a bass
clarinet and all the workings your fingers

work well to obliterate into confidence
and ease. To hold, even, a blood count

in the hat of Mingus in each of his four seeds
is equivalent to a silk wavering in the throat,

to a slurry of bees. To shout back
at him *African, German, Chinese, and Swede.*

To cry out, *Let me die, alone, in some Berlin
hotel*, without the single weeping of a whale,

says diabetes, says what is silent
can kill with the skill of a hundred men.

What love did *you* have in that narrow room, I wonder?
How many tongues could you not speak? For thirteen minutes

thirty-four seconds you're not alone
anymore. Even as I listen, peeling back sugary regret

at the sink. Even as I compost the skin into the mold
of a fragrant heap. How can I ever just *be*? *See*?

How can your certain shade of orange spread before the breath
of my *own* circular breathe? Bactrian brother. Old grain and the seed.

Lost ruby in my throat. What love did you not quite speak?
What of us, of me, did your death repeat?

Even the blind camel kneeling in desert moon
offers up its humps as a partial mirror of the sea.

Dreaming Oneself Dead

with a first line by Jack Spicer

They dream they dream of dreams about themselves.

    1. my killing of an ant when I was six
    2. rain in my mother's throat

    1. I am a woman
    2. the world is dead

You are awash with the eucalyptus offerings of otters.
They dream of black ants dreaming of a mother's release.
Ectoplasm in an epaulet.
A long time from now, all my weeds
will be gone, and houses will tilt upright.
Livers will run amuck. Hybrid lollipops will con each
    dinner napkin
into folding like a hand of jacks.

In the face of a queen. In the black biting of an ant.
The world is certainly dead or dying or about to live.

Sunlight on the blue-black wave of a crow's wing.

    1. I am like a tiny copper spiral
    2. cutting into myself, I find a great hole
       at the core

We open. We clothe.
Excited. Rooted as a dahlia.

I am inside your delicate chest, your fullest breast.
My dark wing, your breath.

I am always turning toward
and away from the love of those loving me most.

A great oak table holds our hands
as if we touched common work.

We upside down in all we love or hate or in loving live.
The missing words loud as Amazonian drums
turned toward—against—the fierce, the hoped,
the whinging words with which we wince,
calling the dirt, *dirt*. The world, *world*.

On the Death of Miltos Sahtouris
1919–2005

So now I will never meet you, Miltos Sahtouris.
So a long time from now, July 29, 1919, will forever be
   inscribed backwards as my shame.

I will never arrive at your tiny Athens apartment, hat in
   trembling hand.
You will not open the door, squinting me my size, and
   tenderly hand me a fish covered in owl feathers,
   saying, *Surrealism freed me from many things.*

But let's say we *did* meet.
Let's say we sat smoking, and that you opened a vein and
   out came Ethiopian tea.

Let's say the mug held blood.
That in the leaves the poems of Andreas Embiricos and
   Nikos Engonopoulos kept soaking like rags in
   kerosene.

And Miltiades—let me call you *Miltiades*, just once,
   reclaiming from the crows your name at birth—let's
   say that we went hand in hand to Hydra to piss on the
   grave of your great-great-grandfather, giving the old
   war Admiral warm water for his bones.
Let's say the entire island turned out to see that in
   his chest he still carried a goat, that the War for
   Independence could never entirely be struck from this
   bone or that.

Like this sliver of eel fire the birth bag burst to become
 my brain.
Like the weight of Cavafy luring us all to some dark
 Alexandrian corner and trembling hand.

On my shelf, alphabetized in the manner of fire or fish,
 your books separate Ritsos from Seferis.
I see you as a kind uncle, keeping the boys from biting
 one another's wrist, instructing them on the merits of
 a tiny cot in a tiny Athens apartment where one sits
 day after day eating tiny cookies from the little
 neighborhood confectionery on the corner.

It has been written that in your *Poems, 1945–1971* you
 cite precisely 526 colors in 234 pages, that the colors
 of black (105), red (82), and white (56) predominate.
It has also been written—but never publicly revealed—
 that in my dream of meeting you, there are 453
 animals silently roaming the room where we sit
 together and smoke, that in one hour, 43 minutes of
 my dreaming the owl appears (one hour, 13 minutes,
 53 seconds), then the donkey and rooster (16
 minutes, 53 seconds and 12 minutes, 11 seconds,
 respectively), and finally the bearded child (a
 fleeting three seconds).

So now it is getting late, Miltos Sahtouris, and all this
 dreaming adds up to the truth that I can never
 dream, can never quite color the sky—that is—the
 same Chagall-horse blue.
You are dead or dying or about to crumble into your

great-great-grandfather's bones or about to be
reborn as some rare poisonous butterfly from Ethiopia
or Peru or Mount Athos itself. And we will never
meet, my friend, and a lace-trimmed wing will part
the sea lice on my chest as I stand on the shore and
sing, and a long time from now we will still never meet.

Francis Ponge Is on Fire

The match is on fire. No, the priest is on fire. No, Francis Ponge is on fire. Fire gives Ponge his body, gives his silk oyster-cream self brilliance. It is a body alive with eclectic thought, with ocean current. The emanating sparrow secretions from his left ear give his body light. It is dark blood-light, like the moment of birth someone who is dying remembers.

The priest is on fire. His black robes are charred parts of Ponge's heart baptizing this child and that. Someone has eased a starter pistol into the rib, Francis Ponge's rib. Someone says, *Stick 'em up! Drop the baptismal font! Give me your oyster!* It is not unlike the confusion of a night of unrequited sex. *Give me your oyster* is rebutted with the sweaty sheet-tangle of *No, give me **your** oyster*.

The university is on fire. The papers are plentiful stars that are, for once, not snobby but in their fragility are about to be human. The brilliant books are alive with wanton ocean depth, burning flood lamps that dim as they enter the mouths of sharks. It is a depth Francis Ponge seeks in the match extinguished in the oyster's rubber limb, an almost holy singe he exacts with the desperate flicking of a pick each evening between each tooth for the charred star and its scar.

Fernando Pessoa Might Call My Body True

It was like lighting my tongue on fire.
The kerosene rag could not be used for the monthly blood.

It was like entering my leopard body, absorbing the sag of
    each dark star as I muscle-twitched my paw-patched
    self bramble-wise across the savannah toward freedom
    and remorse.
The blood bag could not fill even an empty bell or the
    silver of a word I struggled to maintain.

Sure, Fernando Pessoa might call the cave of my body
    true, might send me out onto the parched streets of
    Lisbon begging bread.
Of course, his hatband contained secret words, phrases like
    cave-light in my mouth and *Fedora Pessoa is a bowl of
    frightened soup* and *Stir my blood lightly with a stick.*

I lost a shoe and closed the night as we almost spoke of
    Portugal and pain, of the sandaled sadness of throat
    slash for chalice and spice in ports as colonially close as
    Goa and Malacca.
Anything could bleed, he told me, *if you speak it just right.
    Any mouth could be sewn shut with the awful alignment
    of saffron and scripture.*

He showed me a photo of a zebra in foal, of blacks and
    whites among the scorched ash of bamboo.
He showed me an Indian woman from Goa who refused
    baptism, forced to watch her husband denuded, his
    penis stuffed into his own mouth.

And we wept together as if *both* lit by kerosene.
And the tongue of our mouth was Christlike, if not exact.

And we cried like a child who has lost her star.
And I held Fernando's hand and felt the tender agony of
    release.

Chromium Bones and Imperfect Precision

Every Note You Play Is a Blue Note

for Johnny O'Neal

Let's say the kindness of the heart mated with a riverbed
of gravel. The offspring, of course, would be

your voice. *Old School,* Johnny. The term, invented
for you. We were born the same year. You in Detroit.

Me in Chicago. How can the only 281 miles between
our birth beds along I-94 have created such space?

You're older than me by galaxies. You are the age
of the oldest love. You move through clusters of stars

at the piano with your Milky Way hands, your fingers
kneading bread. Baking it. Smoothing butter and honey
    across crisp

slabs of toast. It is the warmth of every stage of our most
    basic food
that you feed us. You were meant to caress the keys

inside the soft places we show no one. How'd you know
you were the one born to reach in? Lucky you, when at
    thirteen

you first heard your pianist father play Erskine Hawkins'
    "After Hours,"
and he warned you to never embellish a melody. I'm
    listening

tonight to your gig at Smalls. The gorgeous
"I'm Born Again." And I *am*. Just in hearing

all eight minutes four seconds. Somehow you get me to
 taste what I thought
I could not. A snowslide of stars pouring down a quiver of
 silk. Sorry

if I mix my metaphors, but you confuse both my happy
and my sad. Now I want to cry, four minutes fifty-six
 seconds in.

And you grunt out—Mingus-like—fifteen seconds later,
 an animal
sound I know I was and buried and bathed and would
 have loved

to have asked the world to accept. Slowly,
you bring me to myself. The way starlight dissolves

into night and back again. And back. And I'm here in
 Indiana and there
at Smalls and back in Detroit—all in the same instant—
 thanking the midwife

as she coaxes you from the starlight safe of your mother's
 belly
so you might one day bring that peace out into the world.
 How can I say

I love you, Johnny, when your piano runs already say
there are no words for love except the silence you stir

from blowing snowfields of the inner ear? And I'm *small*
    this evening,
hearing you at Smalls as if all your years of Blue Note and
    Blakey

and Clark Terry and Oscar and Diz were there
only to give you—tonight—to me. For you to praise,

without word this night, how great the star-sounds
from which we all somehow fell.

Tina Brooks, Live at Smalls Paradise, April 1958

> *The name "Tina," pronounced "Teena," was a variation of "Teeny," a childhood nickname.*

So there you are, Tina, blowing bread
at Smalls, reaching, once more, right through

"A Night in Tunisia," this time for seventeen minutes
four seconds. Jimmy Smith, Lou Donaldson,

Eddie McFadden, and—on tubs—the great
Buhaina. And this side sidestreams me back

to the smoke-filled sound of April 7, 1958,
each clinking glass saying New York is enough. Saying,

this, the night before my wife's birth. Lemon rinds
as a cervical cap? Crushed possum testicles

as an aphrodisiac? What solitary bread
sifted loose through you like some yeasty star?

Which is what you do, even now as the minnow
holes in your bones breathe a fierce scar

into the carbon you are. You must have known,
Tina, that no man could live long with the name

of a woman, could climb onto stage
with a possum pouch vibe and, night after night,

brood us back to song, quivering through the smoke
of all our restlessness, brandishing

a sax—that public display of your spine.
Tenor man with the soft-toned tongue everyone

dreams to moan with a voice precise
as rice clarifying speech. It speaks in scars.

It says *no* in more syllables than one, tells me,
Saying yes might one day be enough. That the secret salt

of the families blows a cool blues in early April heat
even in the warmest seam of a shirt cuff

untucked from your strut. In granules with which
the pace of your breath gifts us? *This* wife

of mine, *that* saxy lady friend of yours—
both born under an Aries sky, always

like something about to wail itself to song.
How your lemon-rind music caps more than

sound, time upon time giving both of us birth.
Which is what you are, even after prison

corralled your softest tongue in loud ingots
of *close this, open that*. Even after the Horse

galloped through your wrist, bending away
your young. The way an infant resembles

a very old man. Which is what you are
not, Tina, never will be, preserved now

as you are amidst the cool barroom
applause of 1958 before the earth curved

back upon itself, back upon you and all
your compacted breath as the chrome-slowed

saxophone discs of your publicly breathing
spine. Something about to live

a very short time tonight at Smalls. This shiver
of paradise. Again and again.

Buhaina

for Art Blakey—the original Jazz Messenger—also known as "Buhaina"

Smoker-man stroke, as if the count of eight.
Famous shuffle beat making the drumroll moan.
Sweat, and all that shirt as if the cuffs of night.
As if following a rope unwrapped

from the stomach, snow-blind in a cave. Blakey,
how come every side of yours I dig spills shame?
Somehow the forsythia will never be
the state tree, and sassafras tea can never

calm the peony bowing heavy as death
swans. How'd you know to explain the exchange
of music for mud and take us five days past
your seventy-first year? Your left hand, a rain-

stick of Amazonian perplexity? Your right
releasing a sound that scoops out our stomachs
like bark canoes expelling a crush
of bees? If you took their intestines—

one each from all thirty-four varieties
in England before the Great War—and strung them
together, you could reach the moon anywhere
from Indiana. It's the hum of cat gut

diverting the flow of enzymes in your shuffle
beat, or your goatskin stance converting ram's blood
to fasts? Old man and the seed. What you did,
who you, how, and what more. 1954 is alive

with drive, as if the count of eight,
knowing what we beat stuns us and makes us
the animal we skin. The state tree
varies from fish to fish, depending on the gills,

and sassafras tea may or may not breathe
illusory. Play-shake your stick. Perplex
my rain. Complete mine and yours. Every day
between beats we're about to die

once and for maybe. Over and over, rope
upon rope, the beat we can reach is a snow-blind
cave. Even there your workingman's tough
beats time into animal hides strung too tight to dry.

The Book of Dandelions

I was an official-
looking document, an
inconceivable fire stain
on the ant's back.
Lapsong Souchong tea was terror,
and the pine-smoke
smell reeved through the street.

Then it was as if
a broken toe. As if
ropes. As if wind
in a parrot's throat. As severe
pencils forming a fence
of private stick-figure pain.

There were missing questions.
Nowhere was it written,
What is the exponential acumen of scoriae?
Or, *How many lungfish does the moon
consume in midnight mud?* Or,
*Can the plucked Japanese shamisen
resemble the sound of broiling collops?*

The book lay open on my lap
like a mirror, a razor
unsure of face or leg, border
of word-stubble that contained

the ontological certainty
of an underwater lamp.

I locked in. Explosion
of light in my right pupil
left an enormous flower-
bend through me, its stalk
a singular clock hand
in search of its shorter twin.

Nowhere was it said, *nudicaulous*
or *nugatory*.

Dark document of the lame man's limp,
tongue bound in leather, stitched
with goatskin, with
word. Of the official
ant severed from shame.
Sluggish fire of caffeine
dilating the capillaries
in my lung. To sink your silk
dandelion self into the lead
seconds of any given minute—
seventeen, maybe, or thirty-five,
or fifty-three? To locate dairy's horrible moment
as an onrush of clagged breath?

There are too many hours
in each spiky leaf. Too many
shades of words, sharply
indented milk.

The book lay open
like a slag, a smear,
a retraction of one's past.

Nowhere was it asked,
Which way to the growing truth?
How many moons in the golden yellow dead?

Elegy for McGrath

> "*All of us live twice at the same time . . .*"
> —Thomas McGrath

I brought the zinnia and the rusted combine bones back
  from the dead.
I thought of you with your rough-smoked face, your
  guttural and your cough, the gentle lay of weighing
  your tongue into the world.

Whether it was a blues for Cisco Houston, unstrung with
  cancer, poor at forty-two.
Whether it was lamenting Asia and the American dead.

The possum-eyed working-class girl won your heart.
We saw you through the way you saw us first, through the
  sharp teeth and tendering of sawing a log.

Can I say, in these woods, *I love you*? Can I turn toward
  your Ghost Dance as if I lived in Cheyenne?
Can the buffalo branch, the tree of Lenin and Marx, the
  astrological root of Galileo in all his madness come to me
  as if all I wore was black and you were the inside scar
  of a star?

So it was your grandfather who came to Dakota in 1880
  and traded with the Indians as he freighted from Fargo
  to Winnipeg, driving a Red River oxcart, Remington
  at his side, through the season of mud?
So you never gave up the names, made Martin Dies and
  the House Un-American Activities Committee cringe?
  So a long time from now they might still call you
  Tommie the Commie?

Take my hand, compañero. Bring me the coal fire. Let us praise not the slaw but the cabbage half-cocked with vinegar.
I love you like I love an old road of rebellion, like I love petunias over this grave or that, like I love the chromium bones and imperfect precision of your not-yet—your never-quite—dead.

Frumkin Seeds

for Gene Frumkin, 1928–2007

Basil, green tea, Frumkin seeds, she'd written, on the pad magnetized to the fridge. *What are those?* I wondered. *And how interesting that there even is such a thing as a Frumkin seed.*

I had, of course, just taught Gene's *The Old Man Who Swam Away and Left Only His Wet Feet.* Was he more like Williams or Stevens? we'd pondered, settling for the extra rib he'd brought with him, somehow tossed among the Babylonian dogs. We'd read "Uncle Hymie," "My Parents' China," said how learning English had both given to Gene and had taken away. *A gift* was how he would have told me my young—as we sat together in Albuquerque, in Fort Wayne, in the in-between static grove of the phone. How he learned English, at nine, to retrieve cough medicine for his mother. How his Yiddish tongue would hang about him for decades like a third shoe—something to lean on, perhaps, in the rain, but clumsy, at first, when ailing from town to town.

And we'd read Gene's "My Ginsberg Poem," each of us taking a stanza. *I thumb a ride on the road of your death,* is how he ends. And though I'd read it to myself over and again for at least nine years, it wasn't until we read it together, aloud, that I noticed how the enjambment at the close of each stanza showed how each hitched a ride on the other. How we, in the circle, climbed on one another to guide the poem. To find some home, get through whatever hurt to the secret of our bleed. Jaren and Troy. Jason,

David, and Scott. Molly. Elizabeth, Angie, and Annelise. Dawn. Even the *other* Dawn who was still with us in the empty desk, though she had lost the baby and took an incomplete. A new word smoking up from the pines of how and why December seems so rough for so many of us and for so long. Clusters of organic form, projectivist protocol. Islands of words, of Black Mountain shift. Drift. Word upon stir upon blur.

So it is February again, here in December. Ten months of strain. The note from Eric that Sunday about Gene's possible death. The note from Mary one hour and seventeen minutes later that sent me deep. Months of feeling way too old at fifty-one. Months of remembering the tired of his hand. Our favorite bookstore and his forgotten cane. That age spot on the wrist that year after year somehow seemed to grow.

Frumkin seeds. My writing's no better, whether on paper bag, car seat, or fridge. Drift to drift, rib to rib. I write to Mary Ann, *I love you*, and it looks like, *I soothe you*. I scribble to Scott, *Try to focus on Stevens' technique and not just content*, and it comes out, *sad sad glance of the owl*. I ask Jaren for a copy of her Rukeyser paper for a future class, but my script resembles *basil, tea*, and this strange thing called *Frumkin seeds*—anything, I realize, to keep the tribe alive.

Pumpkin seeds, yes, of course! That's what she meant, this wife of mine who somehow puts up with all I cannot see, with what I can never possibly read. Say. The correct

and the be. How the *I and thou*. How the say-so yes-no.
How the wrong way might one day right, and strands
of all that can never be said. Sad. How Gene and me on
that Albuquerque bench, with Old Town as a metaphor,
and all that gray hair. His yellowing comb-over; my
silvering threads curling down to the splint I call *shoulder*.
Pumpkin seeds, of course. Yes. I know now what she
meant, *means*, what to get at the store, how to ask the
stranger for change, the clerk for more. How to bleed.
How this small circle of poets to whom I must say so long
tomorrow cuts me cleanly deep into a seventy-five-minute
Tuesday and Thursday of somehow sane belief. How this
first December snow will, like Gene, like me, like these
boiling, broiling seeds, eventually go away, flow, breed.

                                                (2007)

The Pharmaceutical Chemist to Whom Sailors Came to Get Their Shiners Leeched

They had been warned to carry water
sufficient for what they would bleed.
Their diffident opiums frustrated
an oblique prospect of moths blurring bone.
How the color green. How the thaw of any
human groanment stiffly fed much belly.
A process of actual perversity
stranged, then started to peel back an unfinished
bark that clawed and grasped much like colonial skin.
How tree skin and scroll. How scrawl he longed.
He could and would and maybe one day might
count his life continually in tens
backwards to the sound of *ah*, or to any
syllable strong enough to recall
the missing beat, hidden musical feet
from his hands. He held them like a bruise,
tenderly and with shame, the way his swamp
tongue, plucked from murky depths, wormed itself slime-
hard, made strange moth movements in the dark bowl
about to be spilled with fins of midnight
goldfish. He had even braved the cold
at Cape Evans one South Pole winter
to bring back embryos of emperor penguins.
These creatures, seen as the possible link
between reptiles and birds, bore dark both and light.
Sunken moons, now, crescented his own
lower lids with dark sparks of almost blood,
though he had never been punched except

with the dumb medicinal knowledge
that these men, adrift, were real. That somehow
his tongue might tell their time away off shore
as any human suffering and blood.
As something not quite water. Not quite tree.
Let the blood. Let the shame.

And Finally, the Brides of Lust

As if this tongue.
As if the threshold.

Once a god.
Now only the cousin of sound.

And then finally there's the cemetery
where you walk off down the aisle
with the brides of dust, a ring
of sunburnt grass by the quiet pond
somehow pocked with ripples of rain.

Because moon blood lifts
and falls through the horse's granite.
Because a simple crawling.
Because pig troughs
and the most sensuous oats.

To contemplate the texture of the rain
and mean, *Oh mother, where is my tongue?*

As if a god.
As if pure sound.

Why are the underarms of every woman
in the world suddenly so terribly erotic?
A thousand stars exiled as scars?
To be sixty-three

and finally discover the source
of fire?

Not breast or thigh
but nearly invisible hair stubble
upon the tongue.

Secret storage cut
of the cord?

Blood-light from inside
an ancient cave
corridor?

Rain in the pit
of a freshly dug word?

Once a god.
Once a god.
Now your cousin thunder.

Worms

> *"'There are worms in my house,' wrote my child."*
> —Hiromi Ito

When did you want it, need it, the car
sputtering like your uncle's
left lung, the cost of blood work
in Fort Collins compared to Fort Wayne,
the dome light suddenly snapping on
when you hit a pothole? Amber light
isn't all it's cracked up to be,
unless, of course, it's pouring whiskey shots
of sunrise through the church's stained glass.
When did the bread fall? When did the yeast
stop? When did the shepherd raise his crook
above his head as if a loyal collie and a warm tongue
weren't enough? When did you begin to feel
the lifting like a worm ripped from the liver
and placed before you as a collapsed kiss?
You may donate mornings at the youth
hospital. You may count the stitches
in your left shirt cuff and forget
that your gas tank contains beach sand,
sea lice, and worms. You may grow thirsts
and crave an aspirin when someone asks you
your age. You may develop a rash
around your eyes from looking too long
in the mirror at sixty-three, hearing *eczema* in the phrase
extreme caution. You may contract a propensity
for snowy nights and card tables and afghans
and hemorrhoids and puzzle slivers
of moon. Once, as a young boy, you thought

how wonderful it would be to stay up past ten,
to finally be a sixth-grader, to smoke cigars,
to have your own money, to drive to Lowell and back
or the prom and kiss Sandy Hunt fully on the mouth,
to vote, to play college ball, to eat
chocolate all night just for the hell of it.
When did you want it, need it, your name
removed from the plaque of that famous law practice,
stripped from the uniform of the French Foreign Legion
during a dust storm somewhere in Algiers or the Sudan,
melting away in black blurry letters
on the back of a baseball jersey baking in film clips
in Comiskey Park sun? You step out into what used to be
considered summer light and feel the weight
as a blowtorch carving cancerous cells
into that mole on your neck, detailed maps of enemy camps
branded into swirls of thumb skin, into blueprints
of your own home. You hear worms stir in the basement,
turn through chert and mulch and unresolved
seed. They reach pleading fingers, serving the moon
back plates of its own blurry blood. It's time
for a change. It's time to accept an Indiana town
as now. It's time to acknowledge that your daily
oats and paper and milk are not a closing argument
for the mute, not a march through the desert
in search of well water and a shaded fort, not a sprint
from second on a ninth inning single in the corner
by Minnie Minoso and a digging for home. And it's time
to toast your bread and exhale
steam into crust with that first wintry bite
and consider that the amber of sixty-three

does not have to mean a valve job
and a rebuilt trannie, or a longed-for kiss
piked through the center and baited on a hook,
or your bloodletting by the local coroner
into cups. What are the worms doing?
you wonder. From where did they come,
and why are they here? You want to investigate
aerobic cycling, take up sesame
noodles, tofu, and kale, eliminate
cookies and cashews, examine
a mirror for once without the hatchet
and the hood. The price of wanting it, needing it,
rung up at the station compared to what you thought
it would cost to grow up and drive your own car
from one county to the next.

Lost in the Animal

Luminous in the Owl's Rib

Lost in the animal, in the thickening wood.
How long has the owl been hissing?

You saw each star in the sky
like moon-glint from tiny tops.
Saw the lightning
bug in a dispersal of evening fires
strike a chord of sunlight
you thought lost. Saw one another
through all flicker of sound.

The beginning and ending of the world
in a crooked elm, poised with a mate.
As if food. As if feeding.
Your silk-bark self, limb by terrible limb.

Wings folding the world
back into dark resin.
Grease-fat voice.
Bark, growth, or disease
eyeing you, unflinching, from the cavity
of a tree. As if from inside
some great lost fire
taken from you one night while you slept
in a world from which, in secret,
you'd already been removed.

Map Points

The preceding account of maternal rat behavior is very incomplete. Take sheep, for example, and diseases like scab, ringworm, and screw-worms. The chimps of Mount Asserik picked lice off of those they loved. The book has a preface written by Vervet monkeys near a crocodile pool at Abuko. A summary written by wind as ripples stippling the pool as it leaves. I know it sounds farfetched, but I have been dead, dying, died for as long as I've been alive. Consider somewhere near the middle of the reserve being somewhere near the middle of the reserve. *He's a scumbag*, I thought. And part of me meant it. I don't care if he *is* a lamplighter. Lamplighters can be scumbags. Part of me felt guilty for not being a possum in this life. Another part was the functioning milk of a map. *Go pout somewhere else*, I told myself. *Go south into the great known*. If you read this poem and don't understand, you must be traveling north.

Blue Bossa

for Kenny Dorham

What does the color blue taste like
as it exudes the inside of a star?
How does a smoke-filled bar explain
the consistency of gnats? From the swamps
of Fairfield, Texas, larvae lulled you
almost whole, till mosquito music made you
confiscate the seed. To backwater
the colors green and red is a retreat
into tonal blue? To swallow
your breath backwards to vowel is exhaling
your very shame? Earthy, elegant,
sophisticated cat, finding your way
as a Jazz Prophet, then a Messenger—all
the way to brother Joe. Henderson
and his heat exchanging starlight for blood.
Your blood. Naked blood. Thin gnat-clouded
breath. Such tender hands, Kenny, such work.
Who would have considered the flagrant
dissolve of color as jazz? The intimate
as a moist display of public pain?
Or were you searching the glooms of New York
for mare tails of smoke lit from within
by the blue haze of your tunes? Bossa man,
blue. Van Gogh trumpeter mellowed thirteen sunflower
notches down. You, with Henderson, becoming *It*.
The vagueness of some word or other
to clarify sound? The imprecision
of color as spiritual incision?
Some scar in your heart, Kenny, crawled blue
cornflower. Said sky and jay. Spoke in turns
both indigo galactic, Sargasso deep.

Lee Morgan: The Sidewinder

A hurry of sensed dark. A woodsmoke
spoking out as rays of moonlight. A *yes*
without a note. Sidewinder man, no gun
or boot sole could crush you. You lived for cornbread,
and you gave us every grain. But what hurt
did you peel in your finger, pressing it
into your trumpet all the way from Philly,
directly into our own secret
bleed? What curry of bells blew hot
from your tongue? Some say it was fire ants
from Namibia mounding round your soul.
That the daughter you never grew slid slantwise
through your throat. Some say the snakeskin boot
of drugs bit you hard, clouded your heart
with a blood count too fast to keep pace.
To die in New York, shot by a girlfriend,
is a reaching toward the note you first sought
as a kid with Diz, then for three years
as a Messenger? A Messenger of *what*, Lee?
Of how all the strain of the world might one day
catch up to you with a kiss, cough up clots
of your own unknowing? I can't bear the weight
of African ants crowding my own tenuous
dust. Edging under the skin as fiery
sand burns through even the toughest sole. Can't
consider the color red as anything
other than the coral stripe
of the sidewinder waiting in heat.
A curry of burnt bark. A gun stroke
spooling out rays of the gentlest

moon. A *yes* without the *no* of *what now?*
Sidewinder man sidewinding us over
and again with all the strain of the world.

A History

"All historians die of the same events at least twice."
—Thomas Merton

Is *a* history something indefinite
or a notch above *b* history?
Ask the Colorado Avalanche who keep
losing parts of themselves in the Stanley Cup
Finals. Some man, perhaps a coat seam
in disguise, cuts wide circles in ice
for fishing, swears crappie are better fried
than squid. But with this unrelenting June
rain, *I'm* fried, like an apple turnover
appearing, uninvited, on the set
of one of those B-Horror *Attack
of the Killer Tomatoes* moments
too costly to be dream. Burnt okra
or snow peas as a golden calf?
First, it's the Crown Prince of Nepal (who will go
nameless because of rain), shooting his family
over the missing or stunted or Maoistly
fabricated love we all want any entire
Saturday evening while home alone,
bleaching a black sock to gray.
Then it's the Homestead grad from Fort Wayne
chasing a lifelong dream with the Reds. I'm
certain there's no connection, could never be
the way I imagined growing up
as I watched *My Friend Flicka* and wanted
nothing more than a day on all fours
in some lush Wyoming pasture. If four white socks
mean a mouthful of alfalfa, so be it.

Who am I to decry the cost
of supplements at the Food Co-op, artichoke
extract especially sooting my pocket?
Lint of money I give to get my liver
cleansed? Who am I to imagine kissing
the cute cashier I don't yet know but dream
in grunts, in chimpanzee shuffle
and auburn braid? She shudders and shouts four
is her favorite number. I'm relieved she doesn't
golf. I've heard the cry of every common
person as confused heads of sunflowers
sinking into my chest, as if June
rejuvenation seeped its dark ink.
Ice fishing in Detroit is a long life away?
A season of crappie disguised as a fluid rib?
Some bone that floats below lice floes
in the urgent drone of my hairy heart?
John writes from DeKalb with news of the strange
"monkey-man" in New Delhi terrorizing
not just tourists. Collective hysteria
claimed a pregnant woman who, sleeping
on her terrace, was woken by neighbors
shouting, *The monkey has come!* The woman
fell down a staircase, died in hospital.
To be four foot tall and feared?
To step out into ceaseless June
rain without opening my mouth, cocking
my neck, conjuring my hidden turkey
self and giving in? Bush blames Clinton's
blaming of Bush. I realize the rhyme.
The way *All historians die*

of the same events at least twice.
Consider how catastrophic a Colorado avalanche could be. How a controlled echo does more than burn. Moses, how Moses could return with tablets at any time.

You Slice Away All That Is Not Vowel

I see your uncovered leg and remember the taste of
    breaded shrimp
You don't look anything like your photo
Your hair then was full
I wanted to eat it
The texture of you and touch
Your breasts resembled my mouth
In the moonlight, seaweed seems to multiply like fractures
There are yogis who have lived hundreds of years on such grass
And after they leave their ground remains holy
You can smell them in the wind, the saffron leaves
Like the children you were before you forgot to sound
You slice away all that is not vowel
You reach into me, through my chest
And know there are no hands
Only a dissolve the wake of bees
Can cure that hardness in your salt
Can come softly as heavy weights or moon-waves at your arms
As your bones go all the way down to the ground
Where moonlight becomes the way you hear
When you lived before

After Ray Gonzalez and I Read Our Poetry, Our Friend Bill Tremblay Complements Our Reading

Moments after we read our poems that evening, Ray heard him say *You're Neruda's two socks!* As if Ray and I were two woolen guard dogs of Pablo's cold Chilean feet, saliva-salving his toes with our poems all these years forward from his deathbed in Santiago's Santa María Clinic. But *I* heard him say *You're Neruda's two sons!* As if Neruda had forsaken the copper miners one afternoon to make love with Matilde Urrutia, his great testicles dropping Ray and me among the living, throwing us back out from the copper caves of primordial starlight, unto the world. And unto the whirl of the world and the world's work.

That was some years, of course, after Mary Ann had scribbled *Pumpkin Seeds* onto the grocery list, and I was certain it read *Frumkin Seeds*, pondering—for at least two days—why we'd need to locate Gene's offspring, which were perhaps his writings, in the long aisles of dread, just after the coffee filters, stevia, and tea. Captain Crunch and the Quaker Oats guy staring at us, mockingly, as we'd stumble shelf to shelf in search of Gene's *Dostoevsky and Other Nature Poems.* John told me once he'd *married* his *mother*, which I thought strangely sinful until I realized he'd taken *another* across river in a canoe, *ferrying* him from the east bank of the Kankakee to the west. No matter which direction our words drain away and wander off in search of, it is always true north when they come from the compass part of the heart to nest in the mouth. At least I *think* they nest there, though I'm told they go there, really, to *rest*. Even the radio doesn't help. Last week I heard "Hello Dolly," convinced Louis Armstrong was saluting Salvador Dalí. Or maybe the Dalai Lama. Ray says I should clean the ship out of my ears, but when I go to, no boats are present, only the bobbing waves of words left there, anchorless, adrift, though my common sense, it seems, must have already left port. Even Bob Dylan doesn't help. I search his words for any answer blowing here to there. Wind within wind. As he keeps wailing *The ants are my friends; they're blowin' in the wind.* And I know their tiny exoskeletons must be pointing the way to the most minute grain of Gobi sand, the how of my life and why.

So when Bill complimented our reading, I wondered why Neruda—or *anyone*—could possibly talk the galaxy out of *two suns* for just one phrase of praise. Why Gene's poems were out there, years after his passing, without the right readers, like lonely orphans beleaguered by birth. Why Neruda's "Ode to My Socks" neglected mention of Ray and me, or why Pablo's fortune teller didn't stir the stars enough with her magnificent scarves to forecast decades ahead, beyond his death. How what she might have seen would have been my poems and those of Ray one day undressing the iron footsteps of Pinochet—who thought he heard things right, banishing all confusion to death squads in soccer stadiums—and slipping our wool-warm words, instead, onto the tender skin of Neruda's feet. There, to soothe his toes, freshly torn—as they were—from that soil which seems to have sprouted not just his beauty and his blood, but our timbre and our tongues, giving us syllabic seeds and a dearth of words we might call birth.

The Urologist's Daughter

For a long time I wanted to date
the urologist's daughter. To see if I could
learn what she had inherited
from her father's many probings
of the prostates of others. Would she be left-handed
or right? Would she wear a latex glove
and, while we kissed, passionately
fashion my tongue? Finger me right,
so that I might inhabit our mouth? For a long time,
I wanted gently to stimulate her. Long,
I would divert her focus, lengthening her
soft, most tender, and with that unspeakable place
of my tongue, indirectly
say my name. Up through her
would pass all I had lost or would lose in losing
myself, as might the thoughts of those men biting
their lip, bent against her father's table.
Up through her would pass a world
of desire, like pleasure fish trapped in a net
of air. For a long time I wanted to—
yes—*marry* the urologist's daughter. Then
for a short time, I didn't, then I again wanted to,
and still do, though perhaps not quite. Might she understand—
without knowing—the gripping and biting down hard
of so many men, the how and why
of my inside cry? Could she awaken me
from sixty-three years of my unsteady
steadying of this tongue
or that? Might the urologist's daughter marry
me, bent vast across my lap, *my* table

of hot candle wax and silk, massaging the salty possibilities
of the long-withheld? Milking me
without perfect touch or tongue? Milking,
that is, my milking of *her* from within
the folds of what always remains
hidden, the probings of so many men
pushing forth their tongue into the pain
of surviving, into the unknown
knowing of staying alive.

The Voice of George Kalamaras

after Robert Desnos

So like a scar and a particle of Brahms
my five-pointed want and the shadow of a boy too young
    for divorce
the joyful ache of three a.m., alone, this foggy morning
so like every scar and every prong
it's the far-off cry of a train complaining the track
and the worms in the dirt thrip as if they belonged in
    someone's gut
I crawl to me all those I have lost
an adagio's violin, a taxidermy in my chest, Vallejo's most
    moist, a leopard and a tree
I bleed my name in secret across her dirt
I beg her mammalian face
of rich African veldt, of hyena salt, of the stutter blood of
    a baby zebra breathing its just-stunned past
I hear elephants shuffle as they pass
the tusk of a three-month-dead ancestor who sought a
    watering hole 300 kilometers from its home
I sense urgency in the herd doing the bone-worship and
    how the scent of belonging belongs to us all and etch
    my regret in foreign grass
I call Brahms and his cardigan down from the docks
I call Brahm*an*
I call Vallejo
I call Elytis, Seferis, and Ritsos
I cry for (but do not call) my belovèd Miguel, though I
    refer to him, tenderly and in private, not as *Hernández*
    but as *exact extract of olive root* or *onion tentacle*
    starlight or *scar on my forehead*

the one I want wants joy
the one I want wants joy
the one I want I most simply want
to be born from two parents, reduced to one angry
    mound of table salt on either side of the state line,
    and then grow up wanting to die?
I tug the hypnogogic and the relief
I mouth strange Peruvian skeletal urge
I mouth the condor's wingèd bleed
the predestined collapse of a father's lung precisely at
    12:03 is enough to make a son fear his own birthday,
    thereafter, every December 3
the leopard and the oak cry out for progeny they can
    never bear like Ravi not begetting Mingus not
    begetting Jimi not begetting Jorma
why was the book accepted for publication, after
    seventeen years, the day they scattered George
    Harrison's ashes over the exact spot on which I'd
    meditated a decade before on the banks of Mother
    Ganga?
I receive stares of strangers like exotic house pets
I care for iguanas, salamanders, a baby marsupial still
    worm-pink and screaming the long road of fur across
    its mother's belly after only twenty-six days in the
    uterus
the giving and the dread take up residence in my gut
earthquakes shatter the semblance of my wronged
I want to rock and be rocked
I want to hold and be whole
I want a black silk stocking in the mouth, and I want its how
I want the why of its thigh and the how come

I need the bleed of her name, and I require her to recite
> it backwards three times with her head turned to the
> left, though I don't know whose name she might
> speak and what wing my left arm might become

I want to hatch from one of the only three species of egg-
> laying mammals in New Guinea

I want the duck-billed platypus's electrical find to river food
and the impulse of the current and the male's poisonous
> spur on the leg

I want to paint the walls of my *puja* room saffron and
> sink a pool with carp, only to dismiss the color
> difference between black and gold

I want to sit in perfect *asana,* forget my flesh and—in
> doing so—lay marigolds at the feet of Yogananda

the forgeries of the night express themselves as far-off
> trains, strangers about to couple on the track

something like autumn and damp oak leaves and a stark
> wind make my chest

I expand and induce October in the cool fires of the brain
meditators, through the bone of the toe, listen to my choice
the Ganges, like a snake, unwinds sacred in my mane
the driven and the led declare my grave
cosmonauts conglutinate my asp
I want to include in my broom every speck of lust
keep a cow, a tongue-licked calf, a pack of hounds all
> called *Teach me how not to hurt*

the one I love is inside me
the one I love is near and far
the one I love is a handkerchief and a hurt

We, Among the Living

Wake This Red. Drink the Reach of Grief

for Barney

I wish I understood the rain, the way
it crawls across my shoulder in shadow,
like Gene's death, like Mary's. My female
beagle Barney's final week
and a half when she was too unsteady to eat,
and I poured some strange red juice into her
mouth with a syringe, propped her
from behind so she could pee. That's where I died
for the hundred seventeenth time.
Once there was a storm. Then a boy felt
unloved. We all feel loved when it rains
as if our shadow's shadow were crawling out,
tortoise-tough, to sad weeks and a strange makeshift
gloom, loving us enough to cloak some
magnificent dark. Someone passes you a shawl
with Athenian black-goat fringe, takes your hand,
places her lip into the word you have
yet to speak, the word she creates in body
heat, in two tongues entwined with time
and the minute blood passings too small to eat.
God, I loved her—each one of her—Sandy
from fifth grade. Shelly. Mary Ann,
still. Barney's sad brown eye. I look into the mirror
and believe in God, once and for—maybe.
Maybe, of course, we die *because* we love,
as if loving itself was an Indiana blood
pheasant, a Livermore hawk
talon screaming back the skin, the river-silt
of suddenly seeing through the ripples of this world

and discovering owl resin in the cheek.
I am visited nightly by my wingèd bleed.
I don't come here after November
because the river is dead
cold. People say, *Be easy. Drink the reach
of grief.* People sense this about me when
we meet. This shift of foot, that. The way
I avert my eye from that mole on my friend's
left breast when she breathes—
lovely, low-cut—the rise and
rise of my secret need. Some dark blotch of myself
is always falling out toward me into the eyes
of unrequited love, falling *from* me,
through *her*, through mutual rain. If it's Sunday,
set the table with wild starlings.
If we darken a Thursday, the family
might finally weep. The man in the belly
of the crow is not a piece of bread.
1183 miles of plains
is at least 1184 miles away.
I wish I understood this pain, stretching
its threat like a coral reef paling
its red to dead. First, there's the color
of uncharted weather
crying out to cannibalize itself
with uncertain calm. Then the shimmering
brilliance of touch. Then the rich expanse,
aqua blue. I could die to slide into that ocean
of relegated starlight, and should,
even among Colorado snowcaps. Even
among raccoon hollers, shagbark

hickories, and Indiana
oak. I lost the star-chart,
the figure eight emblazoned
in my chest, when I tried to cover her death
with a green wool vest and standing
straight. God, she was beautiful.
Dark light posing as black beagle fur.
Raccoon mask of a face disguising
the beginning of the world and its
light. The red fluid I squeezed past her
lip that week was my own
inside cry, as if I poured
all the human years of hurt,
the struggle-clutch toward this mouth and that,
into the sun-stung mountains of the West.

Dear troubled dream of being alive—
we are in the body for such a short kiss.
Here, wake this red where rain runs north.
Drink the reach of grief,
the seeps of each waking sleep.

Night Dreamer

> "[hearing Wayne Shorter was] a little like
> being knocked down by a chess player."
> —Brian Case

Let me say the world of your tenor sax is as safe
as a tornado. Let me visit the forever dead
and watch them rise, even as they fall further
into swamp-mouth, grub-head, or ease.
Let me *Speak No Evil*. Let me *JuJu*.
Let me seek *The All Seeing Eye*. Always
let me star-slip, as I do tonight,
listening again to *Night Dreamer* in the rain-
smoke of foggy five a.m. Wayne,
even your sound knocks me down
like moths in the mouth. There's the story
of the king and queen who had no daughters. No sons.
Yet left their world *to* the world. The place
where lonely meets love. A sad shake of hair
a woman bends over you or me or anyone
craving the intimacy of words that never leave
the mouth yet tender the skin with a kiss.
God, I love your moods. Calling forth
their many slants of tongue on "Virgo," "Black Nile,"
"Charcoal Blues," and more. Your opening
solo one minute eleven seconds
in. Where this 1964 set is *now*—
and has always been. *Night Dreamer*
crawls me back even before then into
the solace of a womb world where I knew
all sound and was. And what my mother ate,
I ate. What she touched, *I* touched.

What she said and spoke and speaks.
Even now, still, from her bag of ash.
Your AABA chorus runs are the heartbeat
two lovers formed when they made me
in the in-between. And with your sidemen—
Lee Morgan, McCoy Tyner, Reggie
Workman, and Elvin Jones—you tell me
dead is not enough of a future to behold
when riffs like yours suggest a world.
Let me say the world you make is safe,
even when it's not. Even when it knocks me out.
Even when it stands me in a kingdom of craving
my craving continues to crave. Let me visit
the night dreams your sax sinks into me
and through with a depth only the dark
light of unknowing knows as it tenders
the world *back* to the world. With a kiss.
Forming, unforming. My flesh *back* to my flesh.
Tonight. *This* night. And every night.
In this smoky rain, this five a.m.,
this night dream of what is.

Everybody Digs Bill Evans

> "It's not hard to understand why many Evans followers, 'casual' and otherwise, list it [1958's *Everybody Digs Bill Evans*] as their favorite of the pianist's recordings. It's doubtful there's a more introspective, meditative trio set on record, yet the pianist shows he can dance as well."
> —Samuel Chell, *All About Jazz*

"Peace Piece." "Tenderly." "Night and Day."
Is the world an extraordinary place?
Or is this just trees breathing into us

what we had thought we'd lost to the day's work?
Now the night's moon-leaves leave me three a.m.
blind. There is an owl in my mouth, an owl

in the bony notes you send like mice
icing the keys. Trembling this way and that,
my many molecules might finally make

my mouth. Might stunted and swift the tenses
that tough the tongue into this time or that.
What is past is now. What is now is sound

my mouth only wishes it could make. Notes
flutter me full of possum light this night
that is also morning? Pouched here in what

every animal scrapes down into ground, I dig
deep for parts of myself lost in "Peace Piece."
In "Tenderly." In the forgotten key

of every note you splay and play
and swift into me. As I fall
into my favorite album of yours, Bill,

I fall. Deep. Into the black and white depths
your extraordinary self and the mice
bone you seek keep carving through me.

Mingus Mingus Mingus

> *"In other words, I am three."*
> —Charles Mingus

In other words, a bell grafts the dirt.
In other words, dirt exacts a bell.
In other words, a stirrup of extracted salt.
Which is not unlike tongues of the dead
growing in concert with hair and nails.
Which is not unlike a passel of crows
noising, with brown river silt, a rhododendron.
Which could never be similar to a door
handle unscrewing its glue.
Which could never be granules of *this* and *that*,
yes and *no*, struck to dichotomous heat.
In other words, one plus one plus one
equaling the three sides of a coin.
Which is quite similar, really, to extolling
your life as the size of your instrument,
your heart exhaled as the belly of a bass.
Which is why fifty-six whales beached themselves
on the coast of Mexico the day you died
in Cuernavaca. Which is slightly more than three
times three times three times two
grains of ocean salt.
And so all this adds up to the dead
of a complex man at age fifty-six.
And so any man (or woman) is, finally,
simple. Which is more than can be said
of who, what, when, where, and how. Which
is why we often pursue questions without
correct punctuation, or for that

matter, streets. Which is one way
to have it both ways at once.
Okay, yes, maybe, all right, evidently.
And so in other words, *words*.
And so in other dirt, *bells*.
And so a stirrup of salt in the hand.
And the stirrups of the inner ear
must refuse the secretion of an ovular mouth.
That is, if it seeks your secret blues and roots
dust, the hello and goodbye of your jazz
workshop *moin*, your beautiful
strain just below my, yet still far ahead of its.
Which is why we often sight our questions
with a fierce. Which is one reason a season
in the hand. Which is why and certainly
how, when, and who. *Whom*? Not a sparrow
or hummingbird mood but your beached whale
self, spouting, of course, all kinds of sand flukes
from the belly of the bass. Jonah
and maybe the constant curve
of the term *Charles* housed in a cave.
How a word can and cannot be human.
How it can be as simple as a piano belating the skin.
Which is something similar to a dynasty
of salt. Again and a bled and again.
A halt that occludes its hawk, that catches
the tuft of its tongue on its own accord.
You're expecting from me either love *or* hate?
I hate duality. I love that I can
hate something dichotomous so deliciously.
How it can be as simple as a piano belating the skin.

It's Gone

For the longest time, as an adult, I couldn't say
de Chirico. It kept coming out *de Chiricoo*, reaching
that strange vowel out, perhaps, toward the melancholy

assurance of the lonely girl's hoop.
Nor could I properly say *kielbasa*. It poured out
something like *kala-basa*, sounding less

like a southern slurp on the word *kill*
and more like the opening letters of my last name.
My wife, of course, was embarrassed—more for me

because I'd mostly say these things in private.
Even the custodian at the campus where I teach knew
something was wrong, though he didn't know what,

nor for how long, nor why the contents
of the basket in my office resembled
renegade squids, gusts of thaw-thick primordial ink.

For the longest time I was incapable of saying,
Ritual Poetry and the Politics of Death in Early Japan.
I don't know how, exactly, it came out—nor why

it even *needed* to be said—except slantwise
through my throat as an irrational fear of sperm
clouding the water glass, or as an argument

with my wife over this table setting or that. I tried
unsuccessfully to say *the eternal promise
of everyone's pineal gland*. It didn't *need* saying, I learned,

and matching words to it was like trying to mate
celery and cinder. For the first nine years of my life
I was tongue-tied, with two frenums fiercing

it out in my mouth, the outer one
binding those first years of voice
indelibly into the recesses of my chin. Yes,

at nine, they finally clipped the outer of the two
(the inner one, exposed, alone, left there to bleed). No,
it was not my mother who'd noticed it. Nor my father

who, by then, had gone away. Yes, it's gone.
It's gone now. I think it's finally gone.

Smaller Than What

This quiet in the heart
is not human. It is animal,
vegetal, astral. Light of basil
set burning by a strange hand,
snuffed upward toward your own
and private sky. It is larger
and smaller than what beats green
in the bloody pomegranate seed left
smoking on the table, begging
the Moroccan fruit salad for something
more than orange flower water.
Shape of citrus cooked
by a slow, persistent breath
until it is husked out, its center
driven to a deeper shade of silk.
This is the death
of all things dead.
Yes. We, among the living.

House and Universe

He used to go there once a year, every year
But now he's passed on
And so he doesn't go there anymore
He's moved on to another house the shape of sound
He's a green tree in winter light
Peeling back the years
Shagbark hickory
The vowel of color
That in certain shades lightens a yellow sparrow
To brown
To fluid
Space
He's a tube that cannot hold water
He's not himself anymore but something like her
She's not herself, really, nor him, nor drift of voice
It's not him, nor her, nor shift of rain
Loosening itself into a thunderous calm
But a watery weed the shape of an eel
But ocher robes the dissolve of sound
Like long hair unwinding
Like long hair unwinding
To slice away this heat, this hold

Entering the Corridors of Breath

"1983 . . . (A Merman I Should Turn to Be)"
—Jimi Hendrix

The place between the eyebrows is a path
of sound where moonlight begins. A slow rain rises

and falls in a storm that works toward its
limits: earth, body, land. The dark sea

of leaves draws the willow far down
into the sinking breath, where you begin

again, Jimi, to rise in a September dusk
the lift of a goose-wing sheds over fields

in the sleeper's forehead. A sudden snow-
bank that holds the wolf's slow step keeps

the landscape always drifting north toward
the earth, toward the earth's axis. A small sound

measures the moist shape between a person's breath
and the flesh it seeks, breaking through water,

through the other side of a chant's exile,
through the pyramid you drew that day before you

died, the number nine drawn down within itself
nine times, a merman's descent. But where to look

for heat? How the hum of a stranger's touch
at dusk pieces apart the patience of womb-

water? Fallen roots blossom an electric
earth, a fragrant caravan that wanders off

over the bridge your blues beats through the hills
of Tibet, of Mars, the mountains within unknown

galaxies, a woman's ancient hair. On an island
she waits for you. She strokes your belly, looking far

back through your past into swirling textures
of thought, into a lotus leaf becoming, the way

wood slows to wheat, oil to water. How soul meets
soul. *Soma*, it is raining, Jimi. *Soma mani padma*.

What floats over you in faint earth-howl
holds her left eye steady near your navel.

A thousand suns and moons spiral from inside
each breath the plants ease into the rocks.

The ten thousand things surge from stones.
Volcanoes rise in the sleeper's lost blood.

What heat. The humming clocks of harvest
grain a beat in the hidden symphony against

which a planetary wind defines itself, becoming
border. Buddha-fields pour through trees,

the galaxies of reptile-embrace, a *wind* that *cries
Mary*, a wind where each breath begins

and ends and begins again, dropping a deeper
green in the grass before the falling leaves.

Evening Raga

I've always loved you, since before the first
breath, that embrace that sticks like satisfied hay,
like the unsuspecting stars that darken a wild coat,
a firm insistence between two immense tones,
a persistent wind.

I've loved you over and over in the supermarket
hum of a paper bag, opening, in the meadowless aisles
of grapes touched by women and men I have kissed,
somewhere, once, like music,
in the stranger's glance at dawn that continues
years from now, in front of me.

Because to be born of a leopard and an oak
in a field between two maple leaves
is to hear rain curving the cricket's saw.
Because to leave the stars and drift like sleep
is to hear milk coming
into each unentered sound.

And still, I've held you in my arms
like a forgotten sea,
like a vowel without salt,
like a returning horse who in its kindness lived long
and grew old with us.

I've held you, always, like the ant that continues to die

at precisely 12:03—every afternoon and midnight—
in the curious fist of a boy.

I've held you like the deepening ponds
in pump-house ivy, like a sinking
in the color violet,
like a final thought—
to be born God and not quite God,
to be born bone and not quite breath,
moon, not yet marsh.

Because to kiss the leopard's spots
is to drink starlight
from the dark foreheads of all those
we pass on the street and never touch.
Because to be born between two maple leaves
is to feel the stance of the oak,
unsure of its daylight.

Come to me. Breathe me. Hold my dissolve.

I've always loved you, since before the last vowel.
In name and without name.
In horse and without horse.
In sea and without sound.
In calm and without drift.
In roots of carrots through the rings of Saturn.
In ponds of shifting starlight.
In the long journey of the evening food.
In what comes neither before nor after
the cup of supper coffee whose evening marshes linger.

How
Now the Scar

The Translation of Gratitude

No, not the words *give* or *receive*.
Not, *Here take this tongue*, nor *I will only love you once every other Thursday at nine.*

But the many lives I've led just to arrive, here, at this certain point of sun.
But the cold moon blanching my breath this winter solstice with its strange work of worms.

Paramecia. Amoebas. The cloudy scrawl of deep-water squid.
The Hindu scriptures say it takes more than a million lives just to become human.

All the things I was. Craved. Cave walls. Paint. Buffalo blood. Protozoa of the blood-axe. Centipede pain absorbing invisible sparks of Saturn's torrential turn.
The Bronze Age, splinters in the wheel, even a horse from the Chinese T'ang Dynasty.

Yes, I adore Chinese poetry—Li Po, Tu Fu, Li Ho, Han Shan, Meng Chiao, especially Wang Wei.
Perhaps I once *was* a Chinese poet. If not Wang Wei, then maybe one of his courtesans, the one with the milky white breasts, the one with the delicate wrist and blue rivers of blood—lover of bamboo *in* bamboo.

If not the courtesan, then threads in her open robe.
If not the robe, then a parasite entering her mysteriously from below through the sole of the left foot as she walks barefoot on a dirt floor.

Some part of me is always translated, always inexact.
When I told Mary Ann yesterday, *Shit, it's cold outside*, I
    meant, *How many sleep-breaths have we shared together
    with the dieffenbachia these past forty-one years?*

When I give my beagle her dinner, it's not just *I love you*,
    but *There once was a constellation of a heron feeding
    from my chest.*
Not the words *yes* and *no*, but *black balloon; white, white
    snow of the solstice.*

I look out onto the darkest snow of the year.
Ice fields blister even the whites of my eye.

If I were to give fully of myself without receiving.
If I were to walk among the absent leaves as if the season
    of healing were only a snow squall away.

So we were writing poems in class last winter from a
    common list of words.
Troy gave us *snowberry*, which none of us knew but which
    we all believed delicious.

Lynnanne said *Van Gogh*. Jenni, *linger*. Brian, *daffodil*.
    Laurie, *Canada*.
I can't remember Sarah's word but know it had something
    to do with *salt* and was the one I needed at just the
    right moment.

What simple thing do we need most when we step into
    this body for its brief bout of breaths, finally, and
    become human?

How now the scar, how now our mouths, how now do we
    learn to translate the seductive sway of our own arm hair?

We have lost the olfactory drift of our tails, not by bounty
    hunters in Oregon, as in *Don Coyote*—that poor
    coyote with three legs and no tail I read about in
    a book by Dayton Hyde, bought from two booksellers
    who happen to be two brothers in Fort Wayne named
    Hyde.
We have lost the hidden kiss, the way to be another's
    dearest and most moist—the road of salt and sweat
    and secret hair stubble around the underarm scar I
    would tongue of and lick.

Yes, I eroticize *every*thing. Even the slurping of a bowl of
    North African vegetable soup from the Food Co-op—
    chickpeas, coriander, and the potato's slow roast—
    carried home last Saturday so I could eat it while
    listening to Julia Meek's *Folktales*.
Even the reading of a book about coyotes, as I take it
    tenderly on my lap, in the intimate dark, in that
    certain way, by a certain lamp, near a certain wife and fire.

No, not *give* or *receive*, not *love* or *hate*, never *this* tongue
    or *that*.
Not a translation for *gratitude*, the discourse of the obviate,
    the inexact—not *anything* among the cruel influence
    of dualism.

But the adorable darkness of the darkest night of the year
    consuming me almost whole, as if I am only upthrust
    dust among the fallow seed.

I turn my fierce, my moist, my yet-to-blossom-yet-bowing sunflower self not just *toward* the light, but *into* each brilliant point of that imaginary constellation wading above me in eelgrass, thick and feeding its spooky swamp neck dark into my chest.

The great blue star-bitten heron feeds me, feeds *from* me, like the thirteenth-century Persian poet, Rumi, whose words float still through the ether, who closes a poem with *There are hundreds of ways to kneel and kiss the ground.*
I write this poem with gratitude to each of the ten thousand things that feed me, feed *into* me, here in Fort Wayne near the solstice, as just *one* way to kneel upon, to *heal* that ground.

NOTES

The book's opening epigraph is from Thomas McGrath's *Selected Poems: 1938–1988*, Copper Canyon Press, 1988.

Other epigraphs are from the following:

Jack Spicer (in "Dreaming Oneself Dead"), from *My Vocabulary Did This to Me: The Collected Poetry of Jack Spicer*, Wesleyan University Press, 2010;

Thomas McGrath (in "Elegy for McGrath"), from *Selected Poems: 1938–1988*, Copper Canyon Press, 1988;

Hiromi Ito (in "Worms"), from her short story, "The Pepper Tree," translated by Hitomi Shibata, in *Manoa: A Pacific Journal of International Writing*, Volume 7, Number 1, Summer 1995;

Thomas Merton (in "A History"), from *The Collected Poems of Thomas Merton*, New Directions, 1977;

Brian Case (in "Night Dreamer"), quoted in Richard Cook, *Jazz Encyclopedia*, Penguin Books, 2005;

Samuel Chell (in "Everybody Digs Bill Evans"), from *All About Jazz*, www.allaboutjazz.com, September 4, 2007;

Charles Mingus (in "Mingus Mingus Mingus"), from *Myself When I Am Real: The Life and Music of Charles Mingus*, by Gene Santoro, Oxford University Press, 2001;

Jimi Hendrix (in "Entering the Corridors of Breath"), from the song title, "1983 . . . (A Merman I Should Turn to Be)," from *Electric Ladyland*, Reprise, Polydor, 1968.

"A History of Green" is written after Charles Wright's poem, "Yellow," in *Country Music: Selected Early Poems*, Wesleyan University Press, 1991. The line, "everyone is everybody else," echoes the title of an album by Barclay James Harvest, Polydor, 1974.

"Bangkok Fan (from a Brother Monk)" includes a quote from Thomas Merton, *The Asian Journal*, New Directions, 1973.

"Hiroshima as Inscribed in the Book of Questions" includes (in stanzas four, five, and six) an echo of and a nod to the second stanza of Arthur Sze's poem, "The Unnameable River," from *River River*, Lost Roads Publishers, 1987.

"On the Death of Miltos Sahtouris" includes quoted material (in stanza two) and reference (in stanza eight) to the number and distribution of colors in one of Sahtouris's books, as noted in Kimon Friar's introduction to Miltos Sahtouris's *Selected Poems*, Sachem Press, 1982.

"Frumkin Seeds" includes quoted material from Gene Frumkin's *The Old Man Who Swam Away and Left Only His Wet Feet*, La Alameda Press, 2002.

"The Pharmaceutical Chemist to Whom Sailors Came to Get Their Shiners Leeched" takes its title from a quote during a television interview with Gregory Peck, in which he describes his late father's profession.

"Night Dreamer" includes reference to a few of Wayne Shorter's recordings. Rather than edit the title of *The All Seeing Eye* to include the hyphen for the compound adjective, I have chosen to leave the title as originally presented.

"House and Universe" takes its title from a chapter title by Gaston Bachelard in *The Poetics of Space* (translated by Maria Jolas), Beacon Press, 1969.

"Entering the Corridors of Breath" borrows part of its title from part of a chapter title by Barry Lopez, "Migration: The Corridors of Breath," in *Arctic Dreams: Imagination and Desire in a Northern Landscape*, Charles Scribner's Sons, 1986.

"The Translation of Gratitude" includes a line in stanza six, "a parasite entering her mysteriously from below through the sole of the left foot . . .," which is an echo of and a nod to John Bradley's poem "The Hanged Man" (for Li Ho); and the line in the poem's closing, "There are hundreds of ways to kneel and kiss the ground," is from Rumi, *Open Secret: Versions of Rumi*, translated by Coleman Barks, Threshold Books, 1984.

ABOUT THE AUTHOR

GEORGE KALAMARAS, former Poet Laureate of Indiana (2014–2016), is the author of sixteen books of poetry, nine of which are full-length. He has received several national prizes for his poetry, and he spent several months in India in 1994 on an Indo-U.S. Advanced Research Fellowship. He is Professor of English at Purdue University Fort Wayne (formerly Indiana University-Purdue University Fort Wayne), where he has taught since 1990. He lives with his wife, writer Mary Ann Cain, and their beagle, Bootsie, in Fort Wayne, Indiana.

For the full Dos Madres Press catalog:
www.dosmadres.com

www.ingramcontent.com/pod-product-compliance
Lightning Source LLC
Chambersburg PA
CBHW030055100526
44591CB00008B/158